ODELL BECKHAM JR.

by Jim Gigliotti

Consultant: Craig Ellenport
Former Senior Editor
NFL.com

BEARPORT
PUBLISHING

New York, New York

Credits

Cover, © Geoff Burke/USA Today Sports; 4, © dpa picture alliance/Alamy; 4–5, © Robert Deutsch/USA Today Sports/Newscom; 6, © Johns PKI/Splash News/Newscom; 7, © John Korduner/Icon Sportswire AXA/Newscom; 8, © Beltsazar/Shutterstock; 9, © John Albright/Icon SMI/Newscom; 10, © Tyler Kaufman/Icon SMI/Newscom; 10–11, © Scott A. Miller/ZUMA Press/Newscom; 12, © Rich Kane/Icon SMI/Newscom; 12–13, © Bennett Cohen/ZUMA Press/Newscom; 14, © Tribune Content Agency/Alamy Stock Photo; 15, © Noah K. Murray/USA Today Sports/Newscom; 16, © Evan Pinkus/AP Photo; 16–17, © Tribune Content Agency/Alamy Stock Photo; 18, © Action Plus Sports Images/Alamy Stock Photo; 18–19, © Loren Elliott/Tampa Bay Times/ZUMA Wire/Alamy Live News; 20, © Rich Graessle/Icon Sportswire CGV/Newscom; 21, © Tribune Content Agency/Alamy Stock Photo; 22, © Rich Kane/Icon SMI/Newscom; 23, © Robert Deutsch/USA Today Sports/Newscom.

Publisher: Kenn Goin
Senior Editor: Joyce Tavolacci
Creative Director: Spencer Brinker
Production and Photo Research: Shoreline Publishing Group LLC

Library of Congress Cataloging-in-Publication Data

Names: Gigliotti, Jim, author.
Title: Odell Beckham Jr. / by Jim Gigliotti.
Description: New York, New York : Bearport Publishing Company, Inc., [2018] |
    Series: Amazing Americans: Football Heroes | Includes webography. |
    Includes bibliographical references and index.
Identifiers: LCCN 2017040942 (print) | LCCN 2017042508 (ebook) |
ISBN 9781684025091 (ebook) | ISBN 9781684024513 (Library)
Subjects: LCSH: Beckham, Odell, Jr., 1992– —Juvenile literature. | Football
    players—United States—Biography—Juvenile literature. | New York Giants
    (Football team)—History—Juvenile literature.
Classification: LCC GV939.B424 (ebook) | LCC GV939.B424 G54 2018 (print) |
    DDC 796.332092 [B] —dc23
LC record available at https://lccn.loc.gov/2017040942

For more information, write to Bearport Publishing Company, Inc., 45 West 21st Street, Suite 3B, New York, New York 10010. Printed in the United States of America.

10 9 8 7 6 5 4 3 2 1

CONTENTS

What a Catch!

It was a 2014 football game. Odell Beckham Jr. raced after the ball. Then he leaped backward to catch the pass. Touchdown! Odell had fallen right into the **end zone**. It was one of the most amazing catches in **NFL** history.

Odell is a **wide receiver** for the New York Giants.

Odell's incredible backward catch

5

Sports Family

Odell Beckham Jr. was born on November 5, 1992. He grew up in a sports family. Odell's mom was a star runner. His dad was a **running back**. From age four, Odell wanted to play football, too.

Odell's hometown is Baton Rouge, Louisiana.

Odell with his mom, track coach Heather Van Norman

Odell watched his father play football at Louisiana State University (LSU).

High School Star

In high school, Odell loved sports. He played basketball and soccer. However, he enjoyed football most of all. Odell was fast on his feet and a great catcher. On his high school football team, he became a star wide receiver.

One of Odell's favorite soccer players is David Beckham— another Beckham!

Odell warms up before a high school all-star game.

College Days

Many colleges wanted Odell to play for them. Odell chose Louisiana State University. At LSU, Odell showed off his skills. He returned **punts** and **kickoffs**. Plus, he could catch almost any pass!

Odell catches a ball with one hand!

In 2013, Odell won college football's most **versatile** player award.

Giant Hopes

Odell was ready to follow his dream to the NFL. In May 2014, the New York Giants picked him for their team. Odell couldn't wait to play! However, at practice, he hurt his leg. He spent several weeks recovering.

Odell was the 12th player chosen in the 2014 NFL Draft.

Odell catches a pass
during practice with
the NY Giants.

First Touchdown!

Odell played his first NFL game on October 5, 2014. In the final quarter, Giants quarterback Eli Manning threw a high pass. Odell out-jumped another player for a touchdown. The Giants won 30–20!

Odell caught 12 touchdown passes in 12 games during his first season.

Odell grabs the
ball out of the air
for a touchdown.

Hard Work

In almost every game, Odell made great catches. He made it look easy, even though it wasn't. To become a great player, he trained every day. "If it doesn't challenge you, it doesn't change you," Odell says.

The NY Giants' training camp is in New Jersey.

Odell reaches
for the ball.

17

NFL All-Star

Even though Odell played only 12 games in 2014, he caught 91 passes. He was the NFL's Offensive Rookie of the Year! He did even better in 2015, catching 96 passes.

Odell is known for his amazing one-handed catches.

After making a catch, Odell gets ready to run.

The Next Step

Odell helped the Giants win 11 games in 2016. His next goal is leading the Giants to the Super Bowl. Odell knows he'll have to keep working hard to get there. "Nothing worth having comes easy!" he says.

Odell meets with a group of young fans before a game.

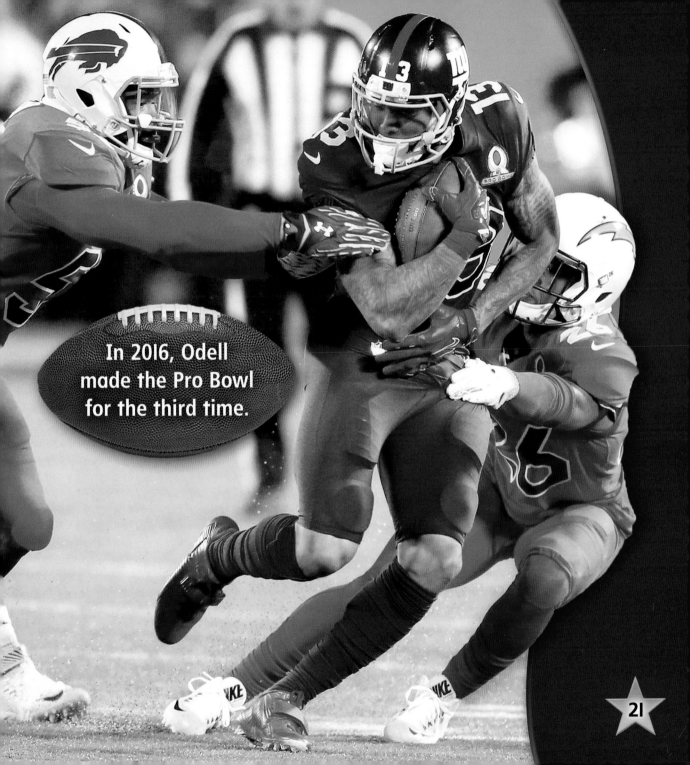

In 2016, Odell made the Pro Bowl for the third time.

**Here are some key dates
in Odell Beckham Jr.'s life.**

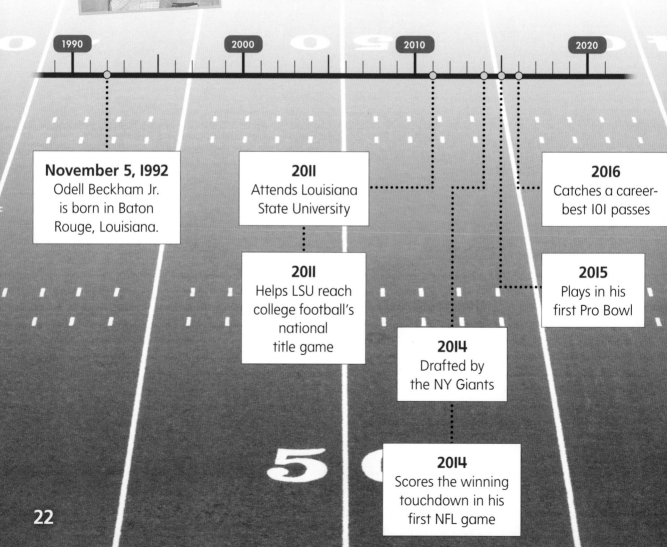

1990   2000   2010   2020

November 5, 1992
Odell Beckham Jr.
is born in Baton
Rouge, Louisiana.

2011
Attends Louisiana
State University

2011
Helps LSU reach
college football's
national
title game

2014
Drafted by
the NY Giants

2014
Scores the winning
touchdown in his
first NFL game

2016
Catches a career-
best 101 passes

2015
Plays in his
first Pro Bowl

Glossary

end zone (END ZOHN) the area of the field where touchdowns are scored

kickoffs (KIK-offs) plays in which a team kicks the ball to the other team

NFL (EN-EFF-ELL) letters standing for the National Football League, which includes 32 teams

punts (PUNTZ) plays in which a team kicks the ball to the other team on a fourth down

running back (RUN-ning BAK) a player on offense who carries the ball and catches passes

versatile (VER-sa-tull) able to do many different things well

wide receiver (WYD reh-SEE-ver) an offensive player who catches passes

Index

Read More

Gitlin, Marty. *Odell Beckham Jr. (Biggest Names in Sports).* Burnsville, MN: Focus Readers (2017).

Kelley, K.C. *Odell Beckham Jr. (Football Stars Up Close).* New York: Bearport (2016).

Learn More Online

To learn more about Odell Beckham Jr., visit
www.bearportpublishing.com/AmazingAmericans

About the Author

Jim Gigliotti is a former editor at the National Football League. He now writes books on a variety of topics for young readers.